ORDINARY
PEOPLE
CHANGE
the
WORLD

I am I. M. Pei

BRAD MELTZER

illustrated by Christopher Eliopoulos

DIAL BOOKS FOR YOUNG READERS

I am I. M. Pei.

I was born in China in the Year of the Fire Snake.
My parents named me Ieoh Ming, Chinese for "To Inscribe Brightly."
But everyone called me by my initials, I.M.

My mom and dad had different perspectives—different ways they saw the world.
She was a poet and flutist who loved the arts.
He worked in a bank.

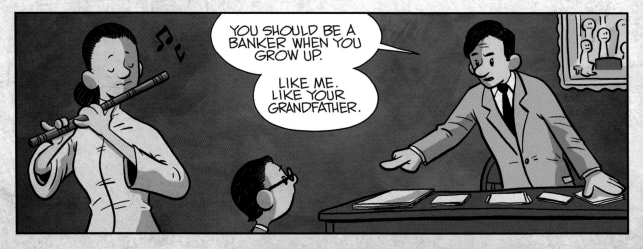

When I was little, my mother took me high up in the mountains. I wanted to explore and run around, but she had other plans—something called meditation.

Just before dawn, I heard a strange creaking, groaning sound:
I thought it was bamboo shoots coming up from the earth!

MOM,
YOU HEAR
THAT?

It was a great gift my mother had given me—to hear the silence.
It let me experience the world in a whole new way.

As a child, one of my favorite places was an ancient garden owned by my relatives, the Lion Grove Garden in Suzhou (which is pronounced "Sue-cho").

To me, it was a giant maze, and I was a marble, ricocheting off every corner.

The way it was designed, you couldn't see a clear path that went straight through.

It forced you to explore and be surprised.

Every few feet, something new would catch my eye.

At the center of the maze were rocks shaped like lions.

But beauty isn't made overnight.

Hundreds of years ago, rock farmers chose certain rocks that they thought had potential.

Then they chiseled and planted the rocks, so water would smooth them over time.

Decades later, the farmers' sons or grandsons would dig up the rocks to finish what was started.

In China, many things were built over centuries, the past and present linked together. The gardens were designed for regular people—artists and poets, not kings and queens.

When I was eight years old, my grandfather taught me about the great and ancient Chinese philosopher Confucius.

He told me, wherever you go, go with all your heart.

I also loved modern things, like playing billiards.
I'd study all the angles, looking for the perfect shot.

When I was ten, my family moved to the city of Shanghai. I'd never seen buildings so tall—ten, twenty, thirty stories high!

When I was seventeen, I made my way to the United States, to study at some of the best schools in the country.

Perhaps the most important thing I learned was this: perspective.
It means the way you see something.
Your perspective can change depending on how you choose to look at an object.
Sometimes, it can happen when you spend time with someone who's different from you.

You can also change your perspective by changing your view.
Zeckendorf had his own plane so we could look at cities in a brand-new way.

It taught me that a city is alive—bustling with activity.

But the best way to change your perspective is to try out new ideas. Throughout my life, I'd wake up in the middle of the night, jot new designs on little sheets of paper, and leave them all over the house.

Not every idea will succeed.

You need to try different things.

After I started my own architecture firm, one of my first jobs was to build a science lab in the Rocky Mountains of Colorado.
To find good ideas, I slept outside the site, listening to the silence, just like my mom taught me.

It was hard. None of my ideas seemed good.
Then, on a trip out to Mesa Verde National Park, I was inspired by the Pueblo Indian cliff dwellings.
The trip showed me their perspective.

The goal was to make the lab look like it was carved from the mountain.

To make the colors blend, we mixed local stones into the building's concrete.

The front path zigzagged like the garden in Suzhou, so you couldn't see it at all until you arrived.

It won Laboratory of the Year.

My real dream, though, was to build museums and concert halls.

Soon enough . . .

I got my opportunity.
In 1964, I was selected to design the John F. Kennedy Presidential Library.
It was one of the hardest projects of my life.
The location moved three times, and critics hated my design.

Mixing old and new—concrete and glass, stone and light—we gave them a space that framed Boston.

When it was finally built, people stopped complaining.

WHOA.

We put President Kennedy's words on the wall:
"All this will not be finished in the first one hundred days.
Nor . . . in our lifetime on this planet. But let us begin."
Like rock farmers, we all must start somewhere.

Not everything I designed was successful at first.
In Boston, during construction of the new John Hancock Tower,
the windows started falling out.

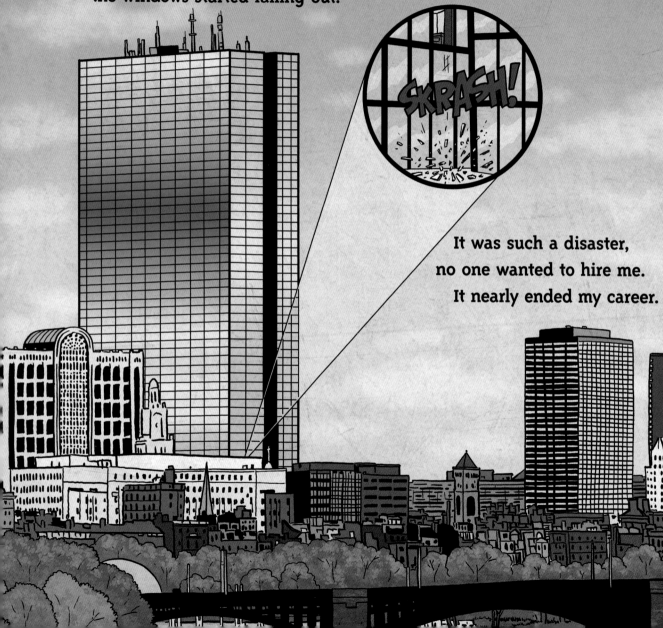

It was such a disaster,
no one wanted to hire me.
It nearly ended my career.

Today, the Hancock Tower is one of the most recognizable buildings in Boston's skyline.
With each mistake, I learned something new.

In time, I was asked to design one of the most famous museums
in Washington, DC: the East Building of the National Gallery of Art.
But the shape of the empty lot was a problem.

For weeks, I tried coming up with ideas, lost in my thoughts.

Even when you draw in the air, creativity isn't magic.
It starts with hard work—and perseverance.

Finally, on an airplane,
I doodled something on
the back of an envelope.

In the first two months, the museum had more than a million visitors. People didn't want to leave, many of them waiting to touch the sharp angle at the corner of the building.

Yet when it came to museums . . .

My most important work was about to begin.

This is the Louvre, one of the most historic buildings in Paris, France, and one of the most famous museums in the world.

IT'S BEEN A MUSEUM SINCE NAPOLEON'S TIME, BUT HASN'T BEEN UPDATED IN HUNDREDS OF YEARS.

WE'D LIKE YOU TO RENOVATE IT.

FRANÇOIS MITTERRAND, PRESIDENT OF FRANCE

The building needed so much work.

Three million people visited every year, but there were only two public restrooms.

MOM, I GOTTA GO!

There wasn't enough space to handle big crowds, or store all the art.

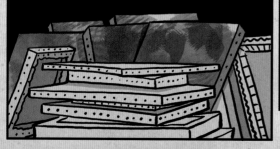

And most important...

HOW DO YOU GET INSIDE?!

No one knew where the entrance was.

It took thirteen years. When critics first saw the design, they hated it.

They didn't want an American, or someone Chinese, altering their heritage.

But when they saw the finished product . . .

Their perspective quickly changed.

Your future is yours to construct, brick by brick.

You can design it, shape it, and . . .

Build something beautiful.

Build something meaningful.

Build something that expresses who you are.

ANTONI GAUDI

BJARKE INGELS

MAYA LIN

I am I. M. Pei, and I know that *you* are the architect of your own life.

"Success is a collection of problems solved."
—I. M. PEI

𝒯imeline

APRIL 26, 1917	1942	1946	1948	1954	1955
Born in Guangzhou, China	Marries Eileen Loo	Receives master's degree from Harvard Graduate School of Design	Joins architectural firm Webb & Knapp	Becomes U.S. citizen	Founds own architectural firm

I.M., age eighteen,
from his student
visa paperwork

Lion rock in Suzhou

John Hancock Tower
in Boston

I.M. at the tenth
anniversary of the
Louvre Pyramid

1961	1978	1983	1986	1989	1990	1995	MAY 16, 2019
Designs Mesa Laboratory at NCAR	East Building of the National Gallery of Art opens	Wins Pritzker Prize	Wins Medal of Liberty	New Louvre courtyard opens	Bank of China Tower in Hong Kong opens	Rock & Roll Hall of Fame opens	Dies in Manhattan, New York, at the age of 102

For our fearless designer,
Jason Henry,
whose wonderful perspective has helped build
and improve this entire series.
B.M. & C.E.

For historical accuracy, we used I. M. Pei's actual words whenever possible. For more of his true voice, we recommend and acknowledge the below works. Special thanks to I. M. Pei scholar Michael Cannell, along with Christina Lenis, Anna Davies, and John Tang, for their input on early drafts.

· ·

SOURCES

Conversations with I. M. Pei: Light is the Key by Gero von Boehm (Prestel Verlag, 2000)

I. M. Pei: A Profile in American Architecture by Carter Wiseman (Abrams, 1990)

I. M. Pei: Mandarin of Modernism by Michael Cannell (Clarkson Potter, 1995)

I. M. Pei: Architect of Time, Place, and Purpose by Jill Rubalcaba (Marshall Cavendish, 2011)

BBC Radio interview with John Tusa (December 2003)

Documentary, *First Person Singular: I. M. Pei,* directed by Peter Rosen (PBS, 1997)

Documentary, *The Museum on the Mountain,* directed by Peter Rosen (Ovation, 1998)

Documentary, *I. M. Pei: Learning from the Light*, directed by Bo Landin and Sterling Van Wagenen (2009)

FURTHER READING FOR KIDS

Build It!: An Activity Book on Architecture by Brian Elling (Smithsonian/Penguin, 2017)

The Future Architect's Handbook by Barbara Beck (Schiffer Kids, 2014)

Iggy Peck's Big Project Book for Amazing Architects by Andrea Beaty (Abrams, 2017)

· ·

DIAL BOOKS FOR YOUNG READERS
An imprint of Penguin Random House LLC, New York

First published in the United States of America by Dial Books for Young Readers, an imprint of Penguin Random House LLC, 2021
Text copyright © 2021 by Forty-four Steps, Inc. • Illustrations copyright © 2021 by Christopher Eliopoulos

Dial & colophon are registered trademarks of Penguin Random House LLC.

Visit us online at penguinrandomhouse.com.

Library of Congress Cataloging-in-Publication Data is available.

Photo on page 38 by Jack Mitchell courtesy of Getty Images. Photos on page 39: I. M. Pei at age 18 courtesy of National Archives and Records Administration, San Francisco; I. M. Pei at the Louvre by Alexis Duclos courtesy of Gamma-Rapho via Getty Images; lion rock by Werner Forman courtesy of Universal Images Group/Getty Images; and John Hancock Building by RhythmicQuietude courtesy of Wikimedia Commons.

ISBN 9780525556015 • Manufactured in China • 10 9 8 7 6 5 4 3 2 1
RRD
Designed by Jason Henry • Text set in Triplex • The artwork for this book was created digitally.

Like the gardens of my youth,
life is not a straight path.
It curves and zigzags,
filled with surprises that are meant to
be explored and discovered.
Wherever you go, go with all your heart.

FRANK
LLOYD
WRIGHT

ZAHA
HADID

Never stop looking at things from different points of view.
Keep your eyes and ears open to the world,
and your mind open to new ideas.

Let the light in.
When you do . . . .